CORE CHEMISTRY

Geological Change

DENISE WALKER

A⁺

Smart Apple Media

an imprint of Black Rabbit Books

This book has been published in cooperation with Evans Brothers.

Series editor: Harriet Brown, Editor: Harriet Brown, Design: Robert Walster, Illustrations: Peter Bull Art Studio

Published in the United States by Smart Apple Media
2140 Howard Drive West
North Mankato, Minnesota 56003

Library of Congress Cataloging-in-Publication Data

Walker, Denise.
Geological change / by Denise Walker.
p. cm. — (Core chemistry)
Includes index.
ISBN 978-1-58340-819-3
1. Geology. 2. Earth—Core. 3. Earth—Internal structure. I. Title.

QE26.3.W35 2007
551—dc22   2006102830

9 8 7 6 5 4 3 2 1

Contents

Introduction

The earth is constantly changing. The continents are drifting on a sea of fluid rock, water is eroding the land, and our climate is warming. We depend on the earth's resources for food, water, shelter, and for building structures and devices that we use every day.

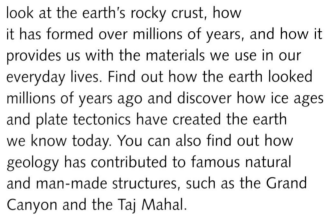

This book explores the wonderful world of geology. Find out how the universe formed and discover how elements were created. Take a closer look at the earth's rocky crust, how it has formed over millions of years, and how it provides us with the materials we use in our everyday lives. Find out how the earth looked millions of years ago and discover how ice ages and plate tectonics have created the earth we know today. You can also find out how geology has contributed to famous natural and man-made structures, such as the Grand Canyon and the Taj Mahal.

This book also contains feature boxes that will help you unravel more about the mysteries of geology. Test yourself on what you have learned so far; investigate some of the concepts discussed; learn key facts; and discover some of the scientific findings of the past and how these might be utilized in the future.

Geology is all around us. Now you can understand how our planet has become the wonder that it is today.

DID YOU KNOW?

▶ Look for these boxes. They contain interesting facts about the geology of the earth.

TEST YOURSELF

▶ Use these boxes to see how much you've learned. Try to answer the questions without looking at the book, but take a look if you are really stuck.

INVESTIGATE

▶ These boxes contain experiments you can carry out at home. The equipment you will need is usually inexpensive and easy to find around the house.

TIME TRAVEL

▶ These boxes describe scientific discoveries from the past and fascinating developments that pave the way for the advance of science in the future.

ANSWERS

On pages 46 and 47, you will find the answers to questions from the "Test yourself" and "Investigate" boxes.

GLOSSARY

Words highlighted in **bold** are described in detail in the glossary on pages 46 and 47.

Formation of the earth

Many scientists believe that the universe was created around 13.7 billion years ago by a fantastic explosion called the Big Bang. This theory states that all matter, space, time, and energy were once concentrated into an unimaginably dense ball, called a primeval atom. The scientists believe that the primeval atom exploded to create our universe.

WHAT IS AN ATOM?

An atom is a tiny particle. Everything around us is made from atoms. An atom contains a central nucleus. The nucleus is made from protons and neutrons. Electrons surround the nucleus.

WHAT IS AN ELEMENT?

An element is a group of atoms that have a unique number of protons in each nucleus. Each element has a specific name. For example, oxygen is an element. Oxygen atoms have eight protons in their nucleus. The lightest elements are:

(1) Hydrogen, which has one proton in its nucleus.

(2) Helium, which has two protons in its nucleus.

(3) Lithium, which has three protons in its nucleus. All other elements have grown from these three elements. Today, we know of 116 elements.

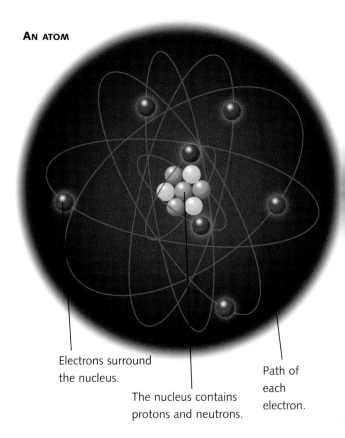

AN ATOM

Electrons surround the nucleus.

The nucleus contains protons and neutrons.

Path of each electron.

BEYOND THE BIG BANG

(1) Scientists now believe that for the first 400,000 years of its existence, the universe was too hot for any elements to form. At temperatures that ranged from several million **Kelvin** to 100 billion Kelvin, atoms burst apart. Instead, the early universe was made of **plasma**. Plasma is similar to a gas, but it is so hot that the electrons are pulled away from the nuclei. A plasma consists of loose electrons and nuclei (protons and neutrons).

(2) After the first 400,000 years, the universe became cool enough for simple atoms to form. Electrons, protons, and neutrons from the original explosion fused together to form atoms. This stage is called "recombination."
(3) The simple atoms began to combine and clump together. Stars eventually formed from clouds of gas under the force of gravity. Any matter that did not form a star revolved around it as a thin disk of dust.

(4) Planets are believed to have formed gradually from these thin disks. The matter clumped together and became more dense until it collapsed inward to form an early type of planet called a "protoplanet." Eventually, the star blew away most of the remains of the thin disk, leaving a planet behind. Planets grew larger as they collided and fused with other bodies.

(5) Earth formed around 4.6 billion years ago. It was initially molten, but as it cooled, the outer layer hardened to form a crust. Beneath the crust is the molten mantle. Beneath the mantle is the outer core that is still molten but more viscous than the mantle. Finally, at the center of the earth is the solid inner core.

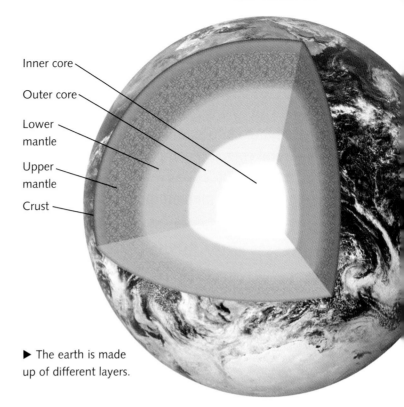

Inner core
Outer core
Lower mantle
Upper mantle
Crust

▶ The earth is made up of different layers.

HOW DID THE FORMATION OF THE UNIVERSE CREATE ELEMENTS?

Elements are formed by **nuclear fusion** reactions. During normal chemical reactions, the outer parts of the atom, the electrons, move to or are shared with other atoms. This forms chemical bonds between atoms to create new substances. However, at very hot temperatures, such as those that exist inside stars, electrons are stripped from the atoms. The nuclei themselves are forced together to produce larger nuclei of different elements.

Even heavier elements are generated from bigger, hotter stars called "blue giants." However, in a star's life there is a point when the star cannot make any more heavy elements. At this point, the star can no longer support the weight of its outer parts. The star collapses in a massive implosion and a shock wave, then it blows most of the star apart. At that split second, the star produces all of the heavier elements, up to and including the heaviest element of all, uranium. This is called a **supernova,** and it distributes all of the star's material throughout the galaxy. Fortunately, the sun will not implode because it is too small. The supernovae of giant stars create many of the heavier elements found on the earth.

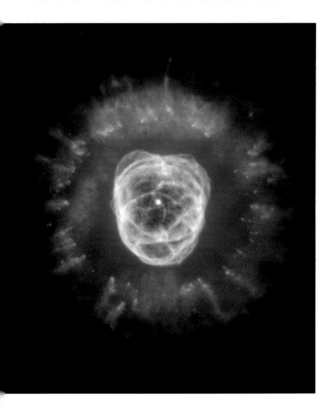

◀ This dying star has formed the Eskimo Nebula. It is ejecting material far into space. It began forming around 10,000 years ago.

The earth's rocky crust

The earth's crust is composed of many different types of rock. Rocks are naturally-occurring aggregates (clumps) of minerals. Minerals are natural chemical compounds formed through geological processes. Geological processes result in three main types of rock: **sedimentary, igneous,** and **metamorphic**.

SEDIMENTARY ROCKS

Sedimentary rocks cover about five percent of the earth's crust and take billions of years to form:

(1) Rocks and the remains of living creatures are broken down into smaller particles by natural forces such as rain, wind, and river currents.

(2) As the rocks become smaller, the tiny sediments can be carried to a place where the natural force no longer operates.

(3) The pieces of rock stop moving and settle. Rock particles that were in liquid solution return to their solid form when the water evaporates. These pieces of rock are now called sediments.

(4) Over time, layers of sediment build up. Older sediment forms the bottom layers and newer sediment settles on top.

(5) Eventually, the weight of the layers compresses the sediment beneath. Under such pressure, the water is squeezed out, and this bonds the sediments. Sedimentary rock has formed.

Sediment can be derived from clay, silt, sand, gravel, or pebbles. Clay produces a sedimentary rock called "mudstone." Its individual particles are tiny. Mudstone that splits easily into thin layers is called "shale." Mudrock, mudstone, and shale form 65 percent of the earth's sedimentary rock.

▼ Layers of sedimentary rock can be clearly seen in the Horseshoe Canyon, Alberta, Canada.

CHARACTERISTICS OF SEDIMENTARY ROCKS

Sedimentary rocks have the following features:

▶ The rock appears in layers in its natural surroundings. These layers represent the different sediments that have been added over time.

▶ Sedimentary rocks may contain fossils. Fossils are the preserved remains of ancient plants and animals. Sedimentary rocks contain fossils, because unlike other rocks, they form at temperatures and pressures that do not destroy animal and plant remains.

▶ On closer inspection, sedimentary rocks have a grainy appearance. If you rub sedimentary rocks between your fingers they may also feel grainy. These grains are the actual sediments that form the rocks.

▶ These fossils are in sedimentary rock that is 8 to 12 million years old.

DID YOU KNOW?

▶ In 2004, scientists studying rocks from Antarctica found a fossil that came from a previously unidentified species of plant-eating dinosaur. The dinosaur was a primitive sauropod, similar to a diplodocus. The dinosaur fossil appears to be at least 170 million years old. The fossil was a hip bone, and from this, scientists concluded that the creature was around 6.5 feet (2 m) tall and over 30 feet (9 m) long.

EXAMPLES OF SEDIMENTARY ROCKS

We call rocks made from the remains of living creatures "biogenic sedimentary rocks." Limestone is an example of biogenic rock; it is mainly made of calcium carbonate from the shells of marine organisms. When the organisms died, they fell to the seabed and created calcium carbonate sediment. Eventually, the sediment became incorporated into limestone rock.

Coal is an extremely important sedimentary rock. It is made from the remains of ancient ferns and trees. When these plants died, their materials were compressed and heated in the earth's crust over millions of years. Eventually, they turned into coal.

Precipitates are another type of sedimentary rock. They form when solutions evaporate and leave the sedimentary rock behind. Gypsum is a precipitate. It is used to make drywall for building houses because it is fireproof. In its natural state, gypsum contains water. When it is heated, the water is released as steam. Its temperature does not rise, and it does not burn until the water has been released.

TEST YOURSELF

▶ In your own words, describe how sedimentary rocks are formed.
▶ Try to find out the names of three more sedimentary rocks. Are the rocks you have found biogenic, precipitate, or neither?

A CLOSER LOOK AT LIMESTONE

Limestone rock, which is a sedimentary rock, forms spectacular outcrops and islands all over the world. For example, the white cliffs of Dover in the United Kingdom (UK), the Niagara Escarpment on the border of Canada and the United States, and the Ha Long Bay National Park in Vietnam, are all formed from limestone. Limestone has a number of important uses in the building industry and in agriculture, and it is the source of many everyday chemicals. But before it can be utilized, **geologists** must extract it from the ground.

LIMESTONE MINING

Limestone is extracted from the ground in a process called "quarrying." Often, limestone is found at sites of particular natural beauty. Unfortunately, quarrying has an irreversible effect on the environment. Limestone is blasted from the ground with explosives. Quarrying in this way creates noise and dust pollution and may interfere with the natural habitats of plant and animal species. However, quarrying can bring employment and much needed revenue to some otherwise impoverished areas.

▼ These magnificent rocky outcrops in Ha Long Bay, Vietnam, are made from limestone.

Once the limestone has been quarried, vegetation is replanted in an attempt to repopulate the area with plant and animal species. The quarry may fill with groundwater, creating a lake. Over time, the natural environment that was disrupted by the mining may be restored.

TREATING THE LIMESTONE

The extracted limestone is heated in a lime kiln. The temperature inside the lime kiln is about 2,730°F (1,500°C). At high temperatures, limestone breaks down into calcium oxide and carbon dioxide. The calcium oxide, sometimes called quicklime, is released through the bottom of the kiln and the carbon dioxide escapes from the top in the form of a gas.

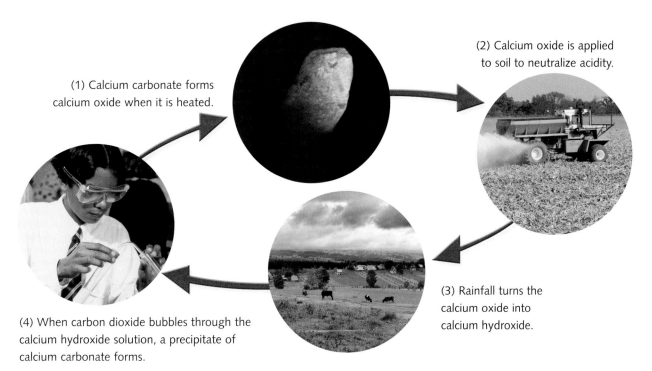

(1) Calcium carbonate forms calcium oxide when it is heated.

(2) Calcium oxide is applied to soil to neutralize acidity.

(3) Rainfall turns the calcium oxide into calcium hydroxide.

(4) When carbon dioxide bubbles through the calcium hydroxide solution, a precipitate of calcium carbonate forms.

REACTIONS OF LIMESTONE

(1) Limestone glows brightly when it is heated to produce calcium oxide, or quicklime. This light was used in theaters before the age of electric lights—hence the expression "in the limelight."

(2) Lime is used in agriculture to neutralize soil acidity. When farmers grow field crops, plants remove nutrients from the soil. This makes the soil acidic. Farmers must replace the lost nutrients and reestablish neutral soil. Lime is an alkaline substance, and when it is placed in acidic soil, the soil becomes neutral again.

(3) When water is added to lime, a new compound is formed. This is called calcium hydroxide, or "slaked" lime. When rain falls on a lime-treated field, the slaked lime sinks deeper into the soil.

(4) When a lot of water is added to slaked lime, calcium hydroxide solution, or limewater, is formed. You may have seen bottles of limewater in your school laboratory because it is used to test for the presence of carbon dioxide. When carbon dioxide gas bubbles through limewater, it turns milky. A pure precipitate of calcium carbonate forms, completing the limestone's reaction cycle.

OTHER USES OF LIMESTONE

▶ **Building blocks**. Limestone is widely available, long-lasting, and easily cut into blocks, which makes it suitable for constructing buildings.

▶ **Cement**. Limestone is heated with clay and calcium sulfate (gypsum) to make cement.

▶ **Concrete**. Concrete is made by mixing cement, sand, and small stones with water. It is a common building material that is used to make foundations for buildings, bricks, roads, and pavements; it also forms a base for fenceposts. Concrete was first invented by the Romans more than 2,000 years ago. They discovered that by mixing volcanic ash and lime mortar with sand and gravel, they obtained a hard, waterproof surface. Without concrete, it would not have been possible to build the Colosseum in Rome, Italy—one of the first buildings to be constructed with concrete—from A.D. 70 to A.D. 82.

▲ The Colosseum is made of limestone, brick, and concrete.

IGNEOUS ROCKS

Igneous rocks are formed when melted rock cools or solidifies. This happens either within the earth's crust or on the earth's surface. Igneous rock formation requires specific temperatures and pressures. The word "igneous" comes from the Latin word for fire, *ignis*. There are more than 700 types of igneous rock, and they make up approximately 95 percent of the upper part of the earth's crust.

ORIGIN OF IGNEOUS ROCKS

The uppermost layer of the earth, the crust, extends 22 miles (35 km) under the continents. Beneath the oceans, the crust is about 6 miles (10 km) thick. Beneath this layer of solid rock, there is a layer of **magma** (molten rock) called the "mantle." The mantle is almost 864 miles (3,000 km) thick and it is constantly moving. Hotter material that is closer to the center of the earth moves up toward the crust; then, it cools and sinks back down. This cycle is called a **convection current**. Convection currents cause the earth's crust to move in much the same way as oil moves on heated water.

As magma moves up toward the earth's surface, one of two things can happen:
(1) The magma can find its way between cracks in the earth's surface and be expelled into the atmosphere. When the **lava** cools, it forms rock that we call "extrusive" igneous rock. This lava is often expelled from a volcano, but it can also seep from cracks beneath the sea (see page 33).
(2) The magma moves toward the earth's surface but does not appear above the ground. Because temperatures are lower just beneath the surface, the magma can cool to form rock that we call "intrusive" igneous rock.

▼ This cross section of the earth's crust shows where igneous rocks form.

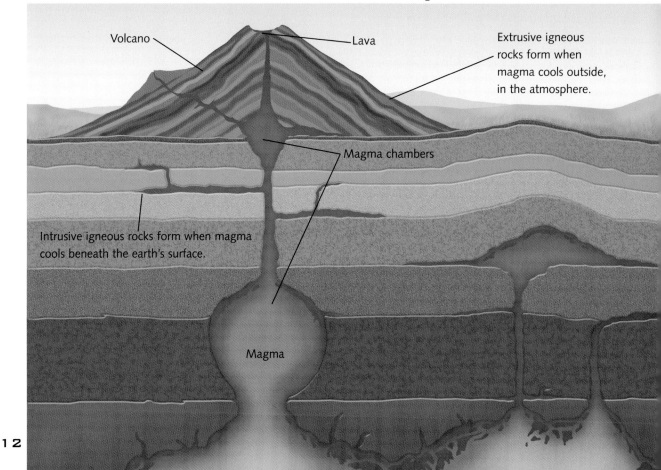

Volcano — Lava

Extrusive igneous rocks form when magma cools outside, in the atmosphere.

Magma chambers

Intrusive igneous rocks form when magma cools beneath the earth's surface.

Magma

IMPORTANCE OF IGNEOUS ROCKS

▶ The minerals found within igneous rocks and their location provide clues about the composition and the temperature and pressure conditions of the mantle.

▶ Scientists measure the quantity of radioactive elements within the rocks to determine their age. Radioactive elements break down at a known rate. If scientists measure radioactive elements present in the rock, it is possible to calculate its age.

▶ Some igneous rocks are sources of important materials such as tin, tungsten, and uranium.

CHARACTERISTICS OF IGNEOUS ROCKS

Granite is an intrusive igneous rock. It is composed of crystals that form when the molten magma cools under the surface of the earth. The longer it takes the magma to cool, the larger the crystals grow. Intrusive igneous rocks form at warm temperatures, and this is why crystallization takes longer. Granite usually forms in massive chunks, and it is hard and tough. This makes granite ideal for widespread use as construction stone.

Basalt is an extrusive igneous rock. When magma is exposed to the cool temperatures in the atmosphere, it quickly cools, giving the basalt rock a small crystal size. The shape, structure, and texture of basalt depends on how its lava erupted and where it erupted. For example, lava can erupt into the sea or the air; it can erupt in an explosive manner, or it can creep down a volcano as lava flow. Some extrusive igneous rocks are expelled from volcanoes so quickly that they do not have time to form even small crystals. Volcanic glass, called "obsidian," forms in this way.

▲ Granite usually forms at depths of between 0.93 miles and 31 miles (1.5–50 km) beneath the earth's crust.

▼ Columns of basalt form when thick lava flows cool. This results in fractures, usually in a hexagonal pattern.

METAMORPHIC ROCKS

Metamorphic rocks are created when sedimentary and igneous rocks change their form. The word "metamorphic" comes from the Greek words *meta*, meaning change, and *morphe*, meaning form. Metamorphic rocks form beneath the earth's surface. The majority of metamorphic rocks are formed from sedimentary rocks because these rocks are naturally pushed farther into the earth's mantle where it is hot and pressurized. Igneous rocks are naturally pushed toward the outer, cooler parts of the earth, but in some instances, they can turn into metamorphic rocks.

ORIGIN OF METAMORPHIC ROCKS

The earth's crust moves as a result of convection currents in the molten mantle below. During this movement, surface rock can be buried and pushed into the mantle. When this happens, the rock endures high temperatures and great pressures. Under these extreme conditions, the structure of the sedimentary or igneous rock changes, forming metamorphic rock. Marble forms in this way from limestone, a sedimentary rock, and slate forms from the sedimentary rock, mudstone.

FORMATION OF MARBLE

A process called **recrystallization** is responsible for the formation of marble. Recrystallization changes the size of the particles found in the rock. Limestone and marble are both composed of the same chemical compound—calcium carbonate—but their crystal structures are different.

During recrystallization, high temperatures allow the rock's atoms to move more freely. They are not as free to move as if they were in a liquid but free enough to reorganize themselves into a new pattern. The high pressure helps squeeze the atoms into their new arrangements. The small calcite crystals change into an interlocking mosaic of larger marble crystals.

▼ Limestone, a sedimentary rock, has a coarse texture.

▼ Marble, a metamorphic rock, has a smooth texture.

FORMATION OF QUARTZITE

In sandstone, the quartz sand grains recrystallize into large, interlocking crystals to form very compact quartzite. The high temperatures and pressures of metamorphism destroy any fossil material present in the sedimentary rock.

▲ This quartzite crag is perfect for rock climbing.

BUILDING WITH METAMORPHIC ROCK

The Taj Mahal, built in India between 1632 and 1654, is a man-made structure made almost entirely from marble, a metamorphic rock. It took over 20,000 workers 11 years to complete the mausoleum and another 11 years to complete the surrounding wall, mosque, gateway, and minarets (towers). Marble is an ideal building material because it is incredibly hard. The lack of spaces in its crystal structure means that it cannot easily chip or crack, and it will resist damage from wind, rain, and extreme temperatures.

The designer of the Taj Mahal appreciated the hard and heavy composition of marble. He angled the surrounding turrets away from the mausoleum, so if they were to fall, they would fall away from the body of the building, limiting any damage.

SLATE

Slate is another metamorphic rock. When it forms from mudstone, the particles are recrystallized into thin layers that can be separated from one another. Slate is extracted from a slate quarry by splitting the material into thin sheets. Slate makes good roof tile because the thin sheets are hard and waterproof. Unfortunately, slate roof tiles are not hard enough to resist breakage when they fall to the ground, and when this happens, the slate breaks into even thinner sheets.

▼ A 9.3-mile (15 km) earth ramp was built to transport the marble and other materials from the city of Agra, India, to the Taj Mahal construction site.

3

Changing rocks

Rocks are changed not only by the movement of the earth's crust, but also by **weathering** and **erosion**. Weathering is a process that causes rocks to break down when they are exposed to physical, chemical, or biological processes. Once rocks undergo the weathering process, they are vulnerable to erosion. Erosion is the movement of rocks by water, ice, wind, or gravity.

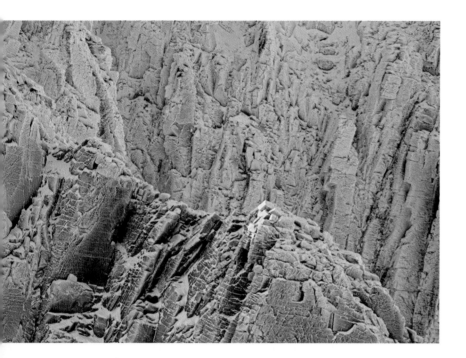

PHYSICAL WEATHERING

A common type of physical weathering is called "freeze-thaw." This occurs in places that have freezing temperatures at night and warmer days. Water seeps into small cracks in the rock. At night, the water freezes and expands. This forces the cracks to open wider and travel deeper into the rock. During the day, the ice thaws and more water fills the expanded cracks. The cycle repeats itself until the cracks become so large that the rocks fracture.

◀ This granite in the Cairngorm Mountains in Scotland has been weathered by freeze-thaw.

Another type of physical weathering is called onion skin weathering, or thermal expansion. In hot desert climates, temperatures vary greatly between day and night. The temperature can range up to 77°F (25°C) over a 24-hour period. The rocks heat up and expand during the day. At night, the rocks cool and contract; this causes stress on the outer layers. Under this stress, thin, skin-like pieces peel off the surface of the rock.

◀ This pebble has undergone onion skin weathering. The outer layer has been removed in places.

CHEMICAL WEATHERING

Acid, water, and oxygen chemically attack rocks. Rain is a weak acidic solution because it contains carbon dioxide from our atmosphere. Sedimentary rocks that contain carbonates are particularly susceptible to acid attack. The carbonates react with the rain and produce soluble and gaseous products. The rock is eventually worn away. As rain water passes through soil, it dissolves the minerals in the soil, which makes the water even more acidic. The effects of chemical weathering can form caves.

Water, acidic or not, can also attack other rocks. For example, when it rains on granite, water reacts with some of the granite's minerals and causes the rock to break down into smaller particles of clay, which are then washed away. This only occurs when the granite is exposed to rain for long periods of time.

Rocks that contain iron will rust when oxygen and water are present. Brown streaks in a rock face indicate that rusting has occurred. Rusting weakens the structure and causes small pieces of rock to break away.

BIOLOGICAL WEATHERING

Plants and trees can take root in small cracks in a rock's surface, even if the crack contains a small amount of soil. Roots grow deep into the

▲ Caves and archways are common in limestone cliffs.

rock, which weakens it and causes it to fracture. Lichens and mosses grow on bare rock surfaces, creating a humid microenvironment on the rock face. This increases the physical and chemical breakdown of the rock.

Animals can also cause rock damage. Burrowing animals remove soil layers that cover rocks. This exposes the rock to physical and chemical weathering. In addition, when animals die and decompose, their remains create a more acidic soil that promotes the chemical weathering of rock.

EROSION

The tiny particles of rock that form as a result of weathering are called sediments. Erosion is the deterioration of sediments by the following forces:

▶ Gravity—Sediments fall from cliffs and landsides.

▶ Wind—Wind carries loose, small, and light sediments such as desert sand.

▶ Water—Crashing waves from the sea or ocean are responsible for the erosion of cliffs and the creation of caves. A fast-flowing river is powerful enough to carry large, pebble-size, sediments. Rivers slow down as they approach the sea or ocean. Sediments are often deposited at the river's mouth, which can cause the river to silt up, forming a delta. When a river deposits sediment, this is called deposition.

▶ Ice—Glaciers can slowly scrape down a rock formation and displace the rock over which they move. Some glaciers can travel three feet (1 m) per day.

▼ The Hubbard Glacier enters the ocean off the Alaskan coast.

DID YOU KNOW?

▶ Geologists have discovered a slab of rock at the top of the Swiss Alps that they believe may have originated from deep in the earth's crust. The rock measures 2,625 by 1,640 feet (800 x 500 m). An analysis of the rock showed that it contains a significant amount of the chemical compound iron-titanium oxide. Usually, this compound is only found deep in the earth's mantle—248 miles (400 km) below the earth's surface. This has puzzled researchers who do not know how this rock came to be at the top of the Swiss Alps.

THE ROCK CYCLE

Metamorphic, igneous, and sedimentary rocks form and change over millions of years. This series of changes is called the rock cycle.

INVESTIGATE

▶ Find out what "porous" and "nonporous" rocks are. Which rock type is best for building?

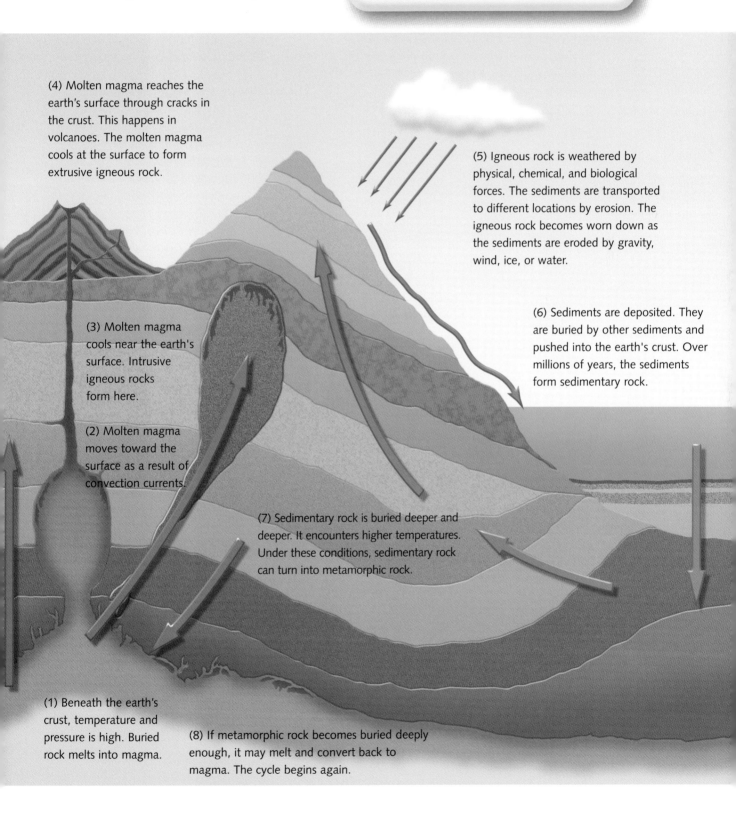

(4) Molten magma reaches the earth's surface through cracks in the crust. This happens in volcanoes. The molten magma cools at the surface to form extrusive igneous rock.

(5) Igneous rock is weathered by physical, chemical, and biological forces. The sediments are transported to different locations by erosion. The igneous rock becomes worn down as the sediments are eroded by gravity, wind, ice, or water.

(3) Molten magma cools near the earth's surface. Intrusive igneous rocks form here.

(6) Sediments are deposited. They are buried by other sediments and pushed into the earth's crust. Over millions of years, the sediments form sedimentary rock.

(2) Molten magma moves toward the surface as a result of convection currents.

(7) Sedimentary rock is buried deeper and deeper. It encounters higher temperatures. Under these conditions, sedimentary rock can turn into metamorphic rock.

(1) Beneath the earth's crust, temperature and pressure is high. Buried rock melts into magma.

(8) If metamorphic rock becomes buried deeply enough, it may melt and convert back to magma. The cycle begins again.

TIME TRAVEL: THE GRAND CANYON

The Grand Canyon in Arizona is around 277 miles (446 km) long, 18 miles (29 km) wide, and nearly 1 mile (1.6 km) deep. A series of sedimentary rock layers forms the canyon. The oldest layers date back 1.7 billion years; these rocks are exposed at the very bottom of the canyon. But how did the interesting rock strata, canyon shape, and vivid colors of the Grand Canyon actually form?

Only five of the ten men finished the difficult journey. Powell confirmed his theory that the river had existed before the canyon and that it had cut its way through the rock to form the canyon. In 1871, Powell explored the canyon again, this time drawing the first accurate map of the area.

FORMATION OF THE SEDIMENTARY ROCK

The exact details regarding the formation of the Grand Canyon are still highly controversial and debated by geologists. The layers of sedimentary rock are believed to have formed mostly below sea level, between 230 million and 2 billion years ago. Warm shallow seas and swamps deposited layers of mud, sand, and lime as the Colorado River's shoreline repeatedly advanced and retreated. The rock layers became compressed and "folded." Limestone from the shells of sea animals as well as fossils of trilobites, marine worms, and jellyfish can be found in the canyon's rock. At one time, there was even a desert in the area that deposited a layer of sand. This has since been compressed into sandstone.

▲ Sunset at the Grand Canyon highlights the sedimentary rock layers.

THE FIRST EXPLORATION

In 1869, the geologist John Wesley Powell took a legendary journey down the Colorado River. He was the first person to study the canyon. Powell took nine men, four boats, and supplies for ten months down the river. When it rained, the river ran thick with red sediment carried by the tributaries that joined the main channel of the river. It was a perilous journey that took three months to complete.

The uppermost layers of the canyon contain red rock produced from shale, siltstone, and sandstone. Some of the layers contain impressions of fern leaves, raindrops, and insect wings. The red color is produced by the presence of iron oxide compounds that have leached out of other rocks and run down the side of the canyon, staining the rock beneath. The very top layers contain a lot of sandstone. Some of the sand particles were transported to the canyon by the wind and helped form the sandstone layers.

▲ The Colorado River cuts through the Grand Canyon.

UPLIFT AND EROSION

Around 65 million years ago, the Colorado Plateau began to be pushed upward as a result of the movement of the earth's crust (see pages 32–35). As the crust moved, the rock was raised, and then squeezed, in a process called "folding." The uplift of the plateau caused the flow of the Colorado River to accelerate, which caused it to cut through the rock more rapidly. The 1,450-mile-long (2,334 km) Colorado River begins its journey in the Rocky Mountains and travels all the way to the Gulf of California. During the ice ages (see pages 40–41), the wetter conditions allowed the river to cut through the rock faster and deeper. Most of the canyon's depth was achieved between 1.2 and 5.3 million years ago.

THE CANYON TODAY

The Colorado River still cuts across the canyon floor, creating a narrow valley and eroding the cliff edges on its journey. But the river is not as great as it used to be. Even as recently as 100 years ago, it was much faster and more powerful than it is today. Decades of damming, diverting, and drought have taken their toll. Furthermore, weathering, erosion, and **transportation** are ongoing and scientists cannot be sure what the canyon will look like in the future.

TEST YOURSELF

▶ Identify two layers from either of the photographs of the Grand Canyon and suggest how each layer could have formed.

4

Resources from the earth

Our planet, and the atmosphere that surrounds it, provide us with all we need to eat, drink, breathe, construct buildings, build computers, and fuel our vehicles. While we often take the earth's resources for granted, our survival depends on them.

MINERALS

Minerals are natural compounds formed through geological processes. There are currently more than 4,000 known minerals on the earth. Rocks are aggregates of one or more minerals. Minerals can be pure elements, simple salts, or very complex compounds. To be classified as a mineral, the substance must be a solid and have a crystalline structure. A crystalline structure is an orderly, repeating arrangement of atoms or molecules. Table salt is a mineral and has a crystal structure. In table salt, all of the sodium and chlorine particles are arranged in a repeating fashion. This pattern is called cuboid.

▼ Sodium chloride (salt) crystals form cuboids.

WHERE DO MINERALS COME FROM?

Many of the earth's minerals originate from the molten mantle beneath the earth's crust. Natural processes in the mantle, such as convection currents, cause minerals to move toward the surface of the earth.

MINING

When minerals are present in a rock and in a quantity that makes them commercially valuable, the rock is called an ore. People have been mining ore for thousands of years. The oldest mineral mine is in Swaziland, Africa. This mine is believed to be around 43,000 years old. Early humans mined for a mineral called hematite, which contains iron oxides and sometimes small amounts of titanium. The miners ground the hematite to obtain a pigment called red ocher, which was probably used for painting.

Today, geologists use both geological and chemical clues to locate mineral ores. They use sophisticated instruments to detect changes in magnetism, gravity, and radioactivity. They analyze the chemical makeup of the ground and use their knowledge of the area's geology to locate minerals. If the geologists detect minerals, they mathematically calculate the quantity and quality of the mineral in the area. If the value of the mineral is worth the cost of extracting it, the ore will be mined.

RETRIEVING THE ORE

The two main types of mining are open-pit mining and underground mining.

(1) Open-pit mining is best if the mineral is within 656 feet (200 m) of the earth's surface or if the rock is not hard and strong enough to support a tunnel. Heavy machinery digs and scrapes away the layers of soil and rock covering the ore. The walls of an open-pit mine are graduated into benches, and the walls are sloped at an angle. This helps reduce rock falls. Gypsum, limestone, and sandstone are excavated from open-pit mines.

(2) Underground mining is used if the mineral is buried deep in the earth's crust. Deep shafts called "blast holes" are drilled down into the crust. Benches are cut horizontally into the rock from the main shaft. Small quantities of explosives are placed along the benches. When the explosives are detonated, the ore is dislodged and falls to the bottom of the long shaft. The ore is retrieved

▼ The upper layers of this open-pit copper mine in Utah have been stripped away to reveal the copper ore beneath.

TIME TRAVEL: INTO THE FUTURE

▶ Humans do not only drill into the earth to retrieve mineral resources. An international research team called the Integrated Ocean Drilling Program has been exploring underneath the ocean floor, toward the center of the earth. So far, the team has successfully drilled through most of the crust beneath the ocean bed. They hope to gain clues about how new crust is formed. It has taken 5 months and 25 specialized drill bits made from hardened steel to penetrate 0.87 miles (1.4 km) into the ocean floor. They want to extend the hole into the mantle another 1.46 miles (2.35 km).

using either a conveyor belt or "skips," which haul the rubble up a separate shaft to the surface. Collection of the rubble is either accomplished manually or controlled remotely to prevent injuries.

Underground mines provide hot, dirty, and extremely dangerous work environments. Miners travel deep underground in caged lifts, and there is a constant risk of falling rocks and fire. In the U.S., China, Russia, India, South Africa, and Europe, hundreds of coal mines are smoldering. Because of the size of the fires and their location deep beneath the earth's surface, they are impossible to put out or control.

TREATING THE ROCKS

Once the rocks, such as limestone or metal ores, are removed from the mine, they are crushed and the waste rock is discarded. Often, at least 30

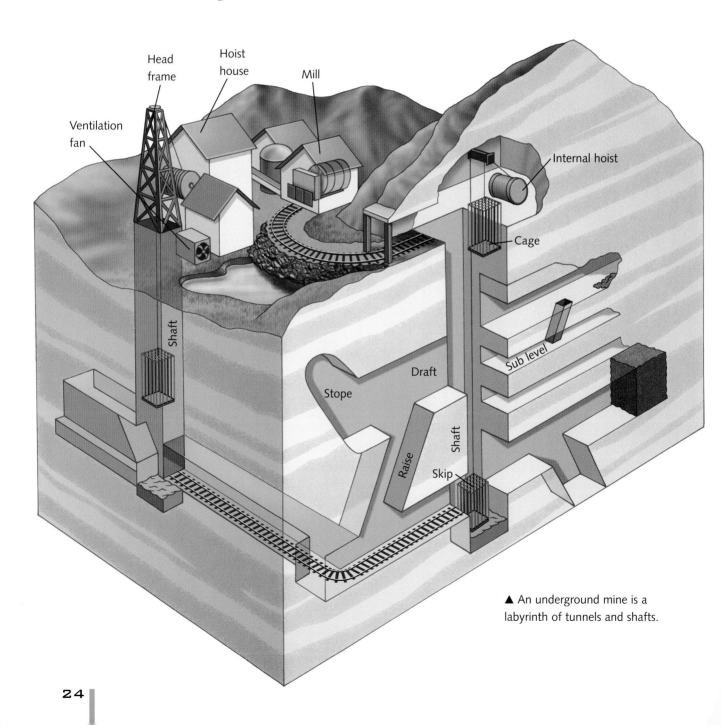

▲ An underground mine is a labyrinth of tunnels and shafts.

percent of the rock is discarded as waste material. The remaining mixture is ground into a gravel-like consistency. Chemicals are added to the mixture to create a "slurry," which is a lumpy liquid. The chemicals coat the valuable minerals so that they float to the surface. The layer on the top of the slurry is skimmed off by a large mechanical arm.

WHAT DO WE USE MINERALS FOR?

According to a survey, the average person in the U.S. consumes about 40,000 pounds (18,144 kg) of minerals every year. In the course of a lifetime this could mean 1,050 pounds (476 kg) of both lead and zinc, 1,075 pounds (488 kg) of copper, 4,400 pounds (1,996 kg) of aluminum, and 999,000 pounds (453,139 kg) of industrial products such as limestone. In fact, we are surrounded by minerals every day. Simple tasks, such as making a pot of coffee, involve a number of minerals. An electric switch may be made from aluminum, copper, and plastic, which is a product of oil. The coffeepot may be made from glass or ceramics, both derived from minerals. The coffee beans may have been fertilized using minerals.

DID YOU KNOW?

▶ ANFO, a mixture of ammonium nitrate and fuel oil, is the main explosive used in mineral mining. This explosive is capable of releasing 110,231 tons (100,000 t) of rock in just one explosion—that much rock weighs roughly the same as 20,000 elephants!

▶ Some plant species accumulate minerals in their tissues. When the Indian mustard plant grows in soil rich in gold ore, it absorbs the gold into its tissues. If the crop is burned and the ash is analyzed, a significant amount of gold can be retrieved. This alternative method of mining has other uses, too. Phyto-remediation is the use of plants to clean up polluted land. Sunflowers, oats, barley, and dandelions absorb strong metal and chemical toxins in the soil through their roots. They safely store the chemicals in their stems and leaves. Eventually, the plants decompose and the soil is cleansed of the pollutants.

▶ **The Indian mustard plant is usually grown for use in cooking, but it can be used to absorb gold from soil.**

The collection of gases that surrounds the earth is called the atmosphere. Most of the atmosphere—78 percent—is composed of a chemically nonreactive gas called nitrogen. Oxygen makes up about 21 percent of the atmosphere. The remaining one percent is a mixture of carbon dioxide, water vapor, and argon. Since the formation of the earth, the atmosphere has evolved (changed gradually) over time.

THE FIRST ATMOSPHERE

The earth formed approximately 4.6 billion years ago from a vast cloud of dust and gas. Its original atmosphere was composed of hydrogen and helium. This is sometimes called the earth's first atmosphere. About 3.5 billion years ago, the first atmosphere was dispersed by the fierce heat of the sun and by the heat radiating from the molten earth.

▼ **This image shows the earth's atmosphere. Earth is the lower dark area. The atmosphere includes the orange and blue regions and gradually disappears into space.**

THE SECOND ATMOSPHERE

As the molten earth cooled, its solid crust formed. However, the molten rock beneath the crust frequently burst through and formed the earliest volcanoes. The volcanoes released gases into the atmosphere including ammonia, carbon dioxide, methane, and steam. These gases formed the earth's second atmosphere, which was primarily carbon dioxide, steam, and a small amount of nitrogen. There was very little oxygen in the atmosphere. Humans could not have survived in these conditions.

Throughout the next few billion years, the earth continued to cool. The steam in the second atmosphere **condensed** to form rain and primitive oceans. Gradually, the oceans absorbed more than 50 percent of the atmosphere's carbon dioxide. The first, bacteria-like life-forms developed. These were the first organisms to consume carbon dioxide and produce oxygen. Recently, scientists have isolated bacteria-like organisms from deep-sea vents at the bottom of the ocean. They are thought to be very

similar to the earliest life-forms found on the earth. Conditions around deep-sea vents, also called underwater volcanoes, are thought to represent the conditions of the ancient, primitive oceans. They have high sulfur and salt concentrations, high temperatures and pressures, and a lack of oxygen.

▼ This black smoker vent is more than two miles (3 km) below sea level.

THE THIRD ATMOSPHERE

During the last 200 million years, the earth's nitrogen- and oxygen-rich atmosphere has developed, forming the third atmosphere. Simple plant life evolved. Plants use carbon dioxide and water in a process called **photosynthesis**. Photosynthesis releases oxygen as a by-product that gradually increased the oxygen content of the atmosphere, allowing more complex life-forms to evolve. As oxygen was released, it reacted with ammonia to create nitrogen. Nitrogen was also released by primitive bacteria living in the soil. In the presence of the sun's ultraviolet light, oxygen molecules combined to form ozone (O_3). The ozone layer protects the earth from the harmful rays of the sun. The creation of the ozone layer protected the surface of the earth from harmful solar radiation, which encouraged the evolution of animal life.

Today, the proportions of gases in our atmosphere are changing as a result of human actions. The levels of carbon dioxide are rising. Carbon dioxide acts like a blanket around the earth and traps heat within the atmosphere. We call this the **greenhouse effect**. On the planet Venus, a natural, uncontrolled greenhouse effect has caused surface temperatures to reach in excess of 752°F (400°C). All of the surface water on Venus has evaporated, which has resulted in high levels of greenhouse gases in the atmosphere. The gases trapped massive amounts of heat and this caused Venus to become extremely hot.

▼ Venus's atmosphere is 96.5 percent carbon dioxide. It contains no oxygen.

USES OF ATMOSPHERIC GASES

Just like the earth's crust, our atmosphere provides us with some important materials that are useful, and in some cases, essential for life.

(1) Nitrogen—The freezing point of nitrogen is almost -328°F (-200°C). Liquid nitrogen is used to freeze many products, including human tissues used for in vitro fertilization. Liquid nitrogen is also used to freeze food, and nitrogen gas aids in food storage. This inert gas will not react with food. For example, potato chip bags are filled with nitrogen gas to protect the chips from exposure to oxygen, which quickly spoils food.

Nitrogen's nonreactivity is also vital for transporting flammable and explosive substances. When oil is pumped ashore from an oil rig, nitrogen gas is pumped with the oil so that the oil is not exposed to oxygen, which could lead to an explosion.

▼ This huge explosion was caused by a liquid petroleum gas leak. It mixed with air, ignited, and exploded.

(2) Oxygen—Oxygen is a more reactive gas than nitrogen. It is essential to the life of all animals, including humans.

(3) Carbon dioxide—Carbon dioxide is used for carbonating beverages. It is a slightly soluble gas and forms bubbles in liquid. When soda cans are left open to the atmosphere, the soda pop goes "flat" as the carbon dioxide escapes. Carbon dioxide can be cooled to form a solid called dry ice. It never forms a liquid at normal pressures, because carbon dioxide **sublimes**. This means that it changes directly from a gas into a solid, without entering a liquid phase. Dry ice is used in stage smoke, because when it heats up, it produces a dramatic, smoky effect.

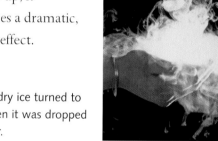

▶ This dry ice turned to gas when it was dropped in water.

Carbon dioxide is also used in fire extinguishers. When applied to a fire, it smothers the flame by depriving it of oxygen.

Under the correct conditions of temperature and pressure, carbon dioxide forms a liquid. Liquid carbon dioxide is used to make decaffeinated coffee. The coffee beans are soaked in baths of liquid carbon dioxide that become saturated in caffeine. After decaffeination has occurred, the carbon dioxide is either drained or the pressure is reduced to normal levels, and the carbon dioxide turns back into a gas.

EARTH'S OCEANS

The oceans cover 71 percent of the earth's surface. Some scientists estimate that the oceans contain 55 quadrillion tons (50 million billion t) of dissolved solids. The oceans contain almost every known element. It is estimated that if all of the salts were removed from the oceans and spread on the land, they would form a layer as tall as a 40-story building.

WHY ARE THE OCEANS SALTY?

On average, three and a half percent of seawater is salt. There are two main reasons why the oceans are salty:

(1) When the oceans first formed, sodium leached out of the ocean floor and chlorine gas entered the water through underwater volcanoes. This formed sodium chloride, which is the most abundant salt in the oceans.
(2) Rivers run across land, and as they do, they pick up minerals. They deposit the minerals in the seas and oceans. Over millions of years, the **salinity** of the oceans increased. The sun evaporates pure water from the oceans and leaves the minerals behind.

Salinity is a measure of the saltiness of a body of water. Salinity varies from place to place, depending on the following factors:
▶ Ice cover
▶ Influx of river water
▶ Climatic factors such as wind, rain, and evaporation
▶ Wave motion and ocean current

The ocean waters with the lowest salinity levels are found in areas where temperatures are cool and where there is a large influx of river water. The ocean waters with the highest salinity levels are found in hot parts of the world, where evaporation rates are high and the influx of river water is low. In addition, polar seas have high salinity because fresh water is frozen into icebergs, leaving the salt behind in the seawater.

The saltiest water in the world is found in the Dead Sea, which is actually a saltwater lake located in one of the lowest exposed points on the earth's surface. The salinity is around 35 percent. The Dead Sea is on the borders of Israel and Jordan. High temperatures and wind speeds increase the evaporation rates. When water evaporates, the minerals are left behind and the sea becomes more and more concentrated. Extensive irrigation and low rainfall in the region have also resulted in high salt concentrations. Salty water is more buoyant than freshwater. The higher the salinity, the greater the buoyancy.

▼ The Dead Sea is very easy to float in because of its high salinity.

RESOURCES FROM OCEAN WATER

Ocean waters are an important source of iodine and bromine. Iodine is a chemical element that is used as a disinfectant, a water purifier, and as a medicine. Bromine is a very rare element. It has leached from the earth's crust into seawater where it is present at concentrations of around 85 ppm (parts per million). The Dead Sea contains the world's highest natural concentrations of bromine at 5,000 ppm. Israel produces more than 198,000 tons (180,000 t) of bromine from the Dead Sea each year. It is vital to the pharmaceutical industry and is also used in fuel preparation, dyes, fire extinguishers, and photographic film.

RESOURCES FROM THE OCEAN FLOOR

Scientists have attempted to mine materials from the ocean floor, including tin, gold, diamond, manganese, and silver. But the mining techniques are currently too difficult and expensive to make sense commercially. The water pressure on the ocean floor is immense and would crush a human.

Today, most of our minerals and resources are still extracted from land despite the abundance of the ocean's resources. There are more diamonds under the ocean floor than there are in the earth. In the future, improved removal techniques may make ocean mining a profitable pursuit.

▼ Salt is evaporated from seawater on the island of Lanzarote in the Atlantic Ocean, 78 miles (125 km) off the coast of Africa.

DID YOU KNOW?

▶ Scientists have discovered that certain species of marine plants and animals can be used to extract rare elements from seawater. For example, cobalt and radioactive plutonium have been found in the bodies of marine crayfish; copper has been found in oysters; and there is gold in the bodies of some jellyfish.

FRESH WATER

Fresh water is found in rivers, streams, and lakes, but it is not evenly distributed around the world. Around two billion people do not have enough fresh water. The United Nations declared a water crisis in 1990. Scientists are trying to find a way to distribute fresh water to places where there are shortages.

▼ This river's fresh water comes from a glacier in Kootenay National Park in Canada.

DESALINATION

Desalination is a process that separates the salt from seawater. Though sailors have obtained fresh water from seawater since ancient times, industrial desalination plants were not built until the end of the 1800s. Desalination was very expensive because it required a great deal of electrical power.

Over the last 20 years, desalination plants have become more efficient and the price of desalinated water has significantly decreased. The most efficient installations can produce 264 gallons (1,000 l) of fresh water for 10 cents. Today there are about 800 large desalination plants in the world, but this is not enough to provide everyone with the water they need, particularly in the developing world.

▶ This desalination plant is near the Caspian Sea.

HOW DOES IT WORK?

There are two ways that desalination works.

(1) Distillation—Seawater is heated and evaporated. Water vapor rises, and leaves the salt behind. The water vapor cools, condenses, and then is collected.

(2) Reverse osmosis—**Osmosis** is the movement of a substance, usually water. The substance moves across a **semipermeable membrane** from an area where there is a lot of it to an area where there is less. In reverse osmosis, the salt water is forced onto the membrane, but the membrane only allows water to pass through it. The fresh water passes through and is collected, while the salt is left behind.

Our changing earth

5

The earth's crust is composed of pieces called tectonic plates. These plates float on the fluid mantle and are positioned like puzzle pieces that do not fit well. The areas of land on which we live are called **continental plates**. The land underneath the oceans is called **oceanic plates**. A tectonic plate can include a continental plate and an oceanic plate. The plates move gradually in a process called **plate tectonics**.

CONTINENTAL DRIFT

This idea was first proposed in 1912 by a German scientist named Alfred Wegener. Wegener proposed that the continents were once joined, but over a period of millions of years, they had drifted apart. We call this idea **continental drift**.

We now know that there are convection currents in the earth's mantle and that these currents move in a circular motion. When solid objects float on fluids that contain convection currents, they move in a particular pattern.

PLATE BEHAVIOR

The earth's crust is made of 10 major tectonic plates and many minor ones. They meet at **plate boundaries**. Tectonic activity, such as earthquakes and volcanoes, occurs at the boundaries. On average, plates drift from one to six inches (2.5–15 cm) per year. There are three ways in which plates move:

(1) Some tectonic plates move toward each other; the consequences of this movement depend on the density of the plates. Oceanic plates are more dense than continental plates, so when they meet, the denser oceanic plate slips under the continental plate. This is called **subduction**. Subduction is not usually smooth; instead, it is sharp, sudden, and violent. This may lead to earthquakes. Earthquakes are shock waves traveling through the earth's crust, and they can have disastrous results (see pages 36–37).

In some types of subduction, the oceanic plate sinks so low beneath the continental plate that the rock melts. Sometimes, this extra molten material leaves the mantle in the form of a volcano. When this happens, the oceanic plate breaks down at the boundary between the two plates. This is called a **destructive boundary**.

A DESTRUCTIVE BOUNDARY

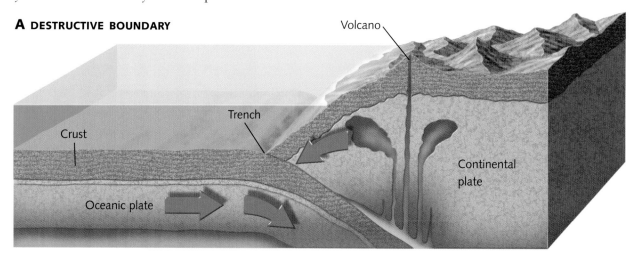

Volcano

Trench

Crust

Oceanic plate

Continental plate

When two plates of similar density move toward each other, the plates collide and push upward. The rock crumbles and folds, producing mountain ranges. The Himalayas are an example of folded mountains.

INVESTIGATE

Find a map in a book or on the Internet that shows the earth's plates and the directions in which they move. Use this information to locate one of each of the following boundaries:

▶ Constructive
▶ Destructive
▶ Conservative

MOUNTAIN FORMATION

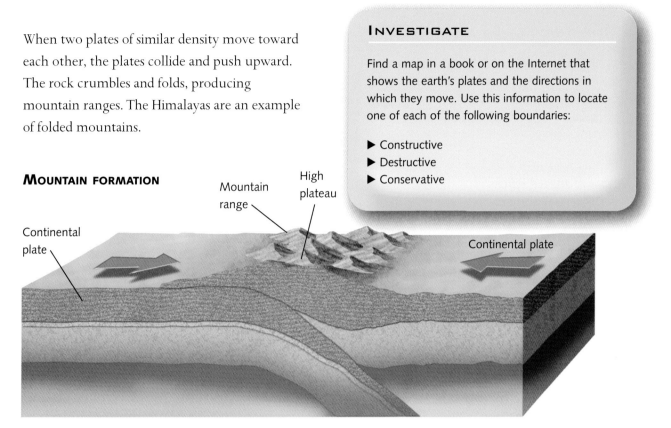

(2) **If plates move away from each other,** molten magma rises to the surface to fill the gap. The magma cools and solidifies on the edges of the plates, creating new rock. This is called a **constructive boundary**. If this process occurs between two oceanic plates, it is called seafloor spreading.

(3) **Some plates move in opposite directions but parallel to each other.** The edges of the plates are rough and the passing movements can be jerky and sudden. This movement might also cause earthquakes. Plates that move past each other in this way are called **conservative boundaries**.

A CONSTRUCTIVE BOUNDARY

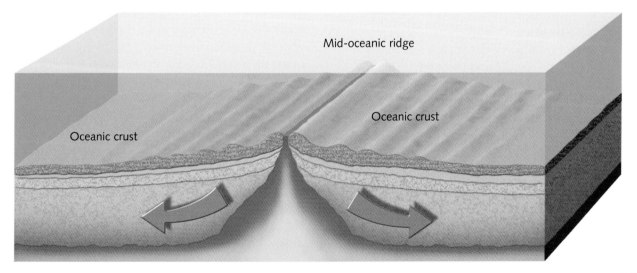

The theory of plate tectonics is widely accepted by scientists. The Pakistan earthquake in 2005 and the southeast Asian tsunami in 2004 are both recent examples of how powerful the plates can be. The following explores some of the evidence for plate tectonics.

JIGSAW PUZZLE PIECES

When you look at the shapes of coastlines, it is easy to see that some edges look like the exact opposite of other edges, like two pieces of a jigsaw puzzle. In 1915, Alfred Wegener published this observation in his book, *The Origin of Continents and Oceans*. He described how the east coast of South America and the west coast of Africa appeared as if they were once connected.

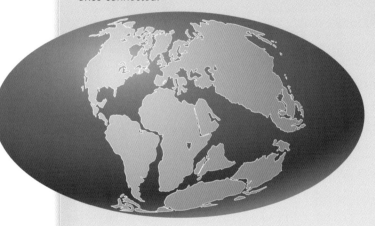

▲ Notice how the coasts of South America and Africa look as though they were once joined. Are there other coastlines that resemble each other in this way?

ROCK STUDIES

Wegener's jigsaw puzzle idea prompted geologists to study rocks on opposite sides of the oceans. They found rocks with identical, yet unusual, chemical structures and magnetic properties. They also studied fossils found in these locations. Elements decompose at a known rate. By measuring the decomposition of elements within the fossils, geologists determined the rocks' age to within a few hundred years. Fossils found in sedimentary rocks on opposite sides of the oceans contained the same species and were the

same age. It is unlikely that these ancient animals swam from one continent to another. The evidence suggests that, in the past, the land masses must have been closer together or connected.

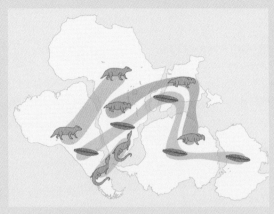

▲ When the continents were joined, animals could easily spread across what are now very distant landmasses.

EVIDENCE FROM THE OCEAN FLOOR

In 1947, scientists discovered that the sediment layer on the floor of the Atlantic Ocean was much thinner than expected. Previously, scientists believed that the oceans were at least four billion years old. If this were true, the sediment layer would be much thicker. The evidence suggests that the evolution of the ocean floor is relatively recent and that it continues to change.

In the 1950s, scientists found a great mountain range on the floor of the Atlantic Ocean. This global mid-ocean ridge is around 31,069 miles (50,000 km) long and more than 497 miles (800 km) wide. It zigzags between the continents, winding its way around the globe. Running along the top of this mountain range is a crack called a rift valley that divides the mid-ocean ridge. It is here that new ocean floor is forming. As the two parts of the ridge move away from each other, magma rises between the plates and forms new ocean floor. This is called seafloor spreading and is an example of a constructive boundary.

In the years following World War II, continental oil reserves were being rapidly depleted, making the search for offshore oil necessary. In 1968, a group of scientists embarked on a year-long expedition, traveling back and forth across the Mid-Atlantic Ridge between South America and Africa, drilling core samples at specific locations. Their findings proved that seafloor spreading was occurring. Ridge samples taken at regular distances were identical in composition and age.

EARTHQUAKES

By the late 1920s, scientists were beginning to identify several prominent earthquake zones. They measured the shock waves produced by earthquakes on a seismograph. This machine enabled them to locate the epicenter of an earthquake. The scientists plotted the epicenters on a map and observed that the majority of them were concentrated along specific lines. They concluded that the earthquake zones correspond to places where tectonic plates meet.

ANCIENT CONTINENTS

Piecing together geological, chemical, and physical data, scientists have concluded that the earth's plates are constantly moving. For millions of years, the plates have separated and reformed several times:

Supercontinent	Date of formation	Date of separation
Columbia	1.8 billion years ago	1.5 billion years ago
Rodinia	1.3 billion years ago	750 million years ago
Pannotia	600 million years ago	540 million years ago
Pangaea	300 million years ago	225 million years ago

▼ When the epicenters of earthquakes are plotted on a map of the earth, the boundary lines of the tectonic plates become clearly delineated.

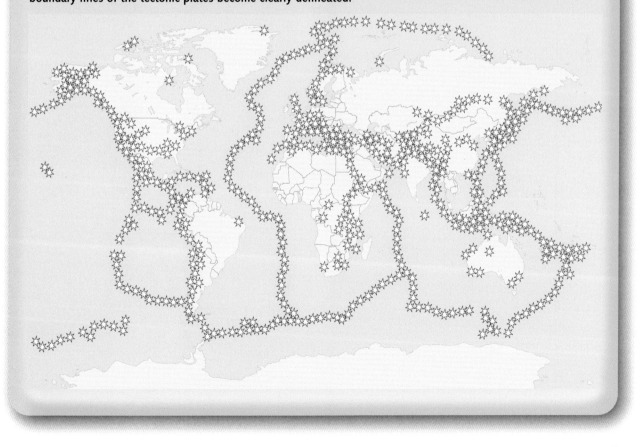

PAKISTAN EARTHQUAKE

It is estimated that earthquakes occur every 11 seconds. Fortunately, most of these quakes are so small that we cannot feel them. But from time to time, massive earthquakes strike. In October 2005, a devastating earthquake hit northern Pakistan. The epicenter was 12 miles (19 km) from the city of Muzaffarabad and 16 miles (26 km) beneath the earth's surface. The earthquake caused widespread destruction and loss of life.

THE RICHTER SCALE

Earthquakes are measured on the **Richter scale**. The scale ranges from 1 to 10. The most powerful earthquake recorded occurred in Chile in 1960. It measured 9.5 on the Richter scale.

THE RICHTER SCALE

NUMBER	EFFECTS	HOW OFTEN DO THEY OCCUR?
Less than 2	None. These earthquakes are not felt.	2,920,000 per year
4	Indoor items rattle. No significant damage.	6,200 per year
6	Destructive. Causes damage to buildings in areas 99 miles (160 km) wide.	120 per year
8	Very destructive. Causes serious damage in areas several hundred miles wide.	1 per year
9 or above	Devastating in areas thousands of miles wide.	1 every 20 years

WHY DID THE EARTHQUAKE OCCUR?

The Pakistan earthquake measured 7.6 on the Richter scale. Northern Pakistan is on the boundary of the Eurasian and Indian tectonic plates. As the Eurasian and Indian plates tried to push toward each other, a massive amount of energy accumulated. The earth's crust shifted suddenly and violently, causing the earthquake. The movement of these two plates over millions of years accounts for the presence of the Himalayas.

The energy from the Pakistan earthquake was transferred through the earth's crust as a shock wave. The shock waves of the earthquake were felt in several cities, including the capital, Islamabad. There have been more than 1,500 aftershocks since the earthquake.

▼ The Pakistan earthquake occurred on the boundary between the Eurasian and Indian plates. The red lines represent the plate boundaries.

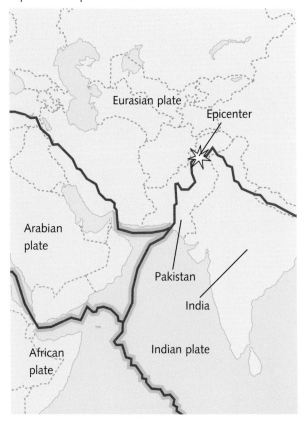

▲ Part of this mountain collapsed when the earthquake struck.

EFFECTS OF PAKISTAN'S EARTHQUAKE

As a result of the earthquake, entire towns and villages were wiped out; hundreds of thousands of buildings collapsed or sustained severe damage; and in the city of Muzaffarabad, close to the epicenter, more than 50 percent of all of the buildings were destroyed. This resulted in the deaths of more than 90,000 people in Pakistan and India; more than 106,000 people were injured.

In addition, the United Nations estimates that around four million people were directly affected by the earthquake. Survivors struggled to cope without shelter, food, or water. Rescue efforts were delayed because of heavy rain, mudslides, and the onset of winter in the mountainous Himalayan terrain. Mudslides carried away villages and buried some people who had survived the initial earthquake but were trapped under rubble.

Another great threat following the earthquake was disease. A lack of fresh water and proper sanitation helped diseases spread quickly. Medication and medical expertise were not readily available. Cholera, typhoid, and tetanus became widespread. The international community donated more than $5.8 billion dollars to help survivors and rebuild the region, but there is still a long way to go.

VOLCANOES

Volcanoes exist all over the world, usually along tectonic plate boundaries. Some volcanoes, such as those that formed the Hawaiian islands, are nowhere near a plate boundary. These volcanoes are formed by "hot spots." A hot spot is an area that has experienced volcanic activity over a long period of time. There is much debate surrounding the cause of hot spots.

HOT SPOTS

There are between 40 and 50 known hot spots on earth. Hawaii, Réunion (an island in the Indian Ocean), Yellowstone National Park, the Galápagos Islands, and Iceland are located over the most active hot spots. Some scientists believe that hot spots are formed by stationary plumes of magma that well up from the mantle and break through the earth's surface. Other scientists have argued that their instruments measure differences in the magma and mantle activity between hot spots. They think that hot spots are caused by plate tectonics, not magma.

Interestingly, the chain of Hawaiian Islands formed as the Pacific plate moved over a hot spot.

This plate moves northwest at a rate of 32 miles (52 km) every one million years. The hot spot has remained stationary, and its eruptions resulted in the chain of islands. The islands in the northwest are the oldest and smallest because they have been eroding longer. The newer and larger islands are in the southeast.

LAVA

When molten magma erupts through the crust, the material is called lava. Lava varies depending on the minerals and gases that are dissolved in it. For example, lava that contains silica is highly viscous (thick), and it will not spread a great distance. When silica is absent, the lava is less viscous and can flow freely over a much greater distance.

The viscosity of the lava inside a volcano determines the volcano's shape. If the lava is thin and flows freely, the volcano will be wide, with shallow sides. These kinds of volcanoes release huge quantities of lava, creating a wide mountain. The largest volcano of this type is Mauna Loa, which forms part of the island of Hawaii. It is more than 13,600 feet (4,145 m) above sea level and is an incredible 75 miles (120 km) in diameter.

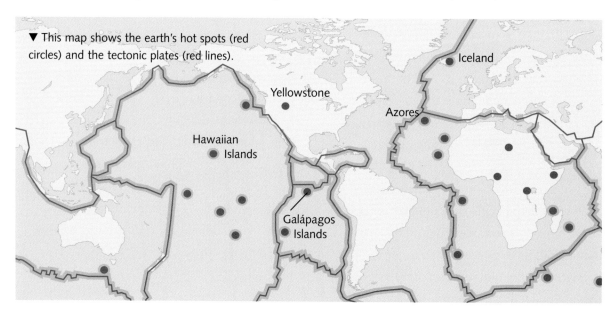

▼ This map shows the earth's hot spots (red circles) and the tectonic plates (red lines).

If a volcano's lava is thick, it does not flow as freely or as far. It builds narrower volcanoes with steep sides. Steep volcanoes are often extremely explosive. The pressure inside builds, and when it is released, a large amount of lava is forced through a narrow space.

▲ Mount Fuji in Japan generates thick lava.

MOUNT PINATUBO

In 1991, Mount Pinatubo in the Philippines erupted with such tremendous force that more than two cubic miles (5 cu km) of material was expelled.

▼ Mount Pinatubo's eruption blasted away 492 feet (150 m) of the volcano. It generated a massive cloud of ash.

The ash was ejected 21 miles (34 km) into the atmosphere. The ash particles rubbed together, which produced static electricity. This formed lightning bolts inside the ash cloud. The lava flowed 10 miles (16 km) from the volcano, destroying buildings and killing more than 300 people. It was one of the most powerful eruptions of the twentieth century. However, compared to prehistoric eruptions, Mount Pinatubo was very weak.

SUPERVOLCANOES

La Garita, a volcano in the San Juan Mountains in Colorado, was the site of the largest volcanic eruption ever. The enormous eruption occurred 27 million years ago on an unprecedented scale. The caldera—the collapsed remnant of the volcano—is 47 miles (75 km) long and 22 miles (35 km) wide, and the explosion is thought to have released 2,000 cubic miles (5,000 cu km) of material. The ash may have reached the east coast of North America, and the Caribbean Sea—more than 1,864 miles (3,000 km). Fortunately, this volcano is now extinct.

DID YOU KNOW?

▶ Lava that contains little or no dissolved minerals can flow over an area of 38.6 square miles (100 sq km) at a temperature of approximately 1,832°F (1,000°C).

GLACIATION

A glaciation is also called an ice age. Glaciation occurs when ice sheets advance from each pole toward the equator. Glaciation is very different from a short-term change in weather, such as a cold winter. Glaciation happens on a global scale over thousands or millions of years. There have been four major periods of glaciation in the earth's history and many more minor glacial periods. The last minor glacial period ended 10,000 years ago, within human history. For the past 700 years, the earth's average temperature has fallen by 3.6°F (2°C), which may indicate the approach of an ice age.

WHY DOES THE EARTH COOL?

The most important factors are:

▶ **Earth's orbit around the sun**—This can change from a circular orbit to a more oval one. If the orbit is oval, the earth will experience very cold winters and cool summers. When the summers are so cool that ice from the previous winter does not melt, this indicates the onset of an ice age. The more ice that covers the earth, the more the sun's rays are reflected back into space off the earth's surface, further lowering the earth's temperature.

▶ **The energy emitted by the sun (solar output)** —Solar output varies with time. When solar output is low, the earth cools. Solar output increases and decreases over an 11-year cycle, but scientists also believe that the sun has activity cycles that last hundreds or thousands of years.

▶ **Natural changes in the proportion of gases in our atmosphere**—Carbon dioxide acts as a blanket, retaining heat in the atmosphere. This causes warming, a natural greenhouse effect. The reverse of this, a decreased level of carbon dioxide, can cause cooling.

HOW DOES THE ICE FORM?

As the earth cools, winter snow remains for longer periods each year. Eventually, the snow cover lasts throughout the summer. Each year, the snow is compressed by more snowfall. In addition, some of the surface snow can melt slightly, and the melted snow seeps into the layers beneath. This fills air gaps and creates a hard, dense ice.

THE POWER OF ICE AGES

Glaciers exert powerful forces on the materials around them. Ice erodes, transports, and deposits sediments, which is similar to the effect that water has on land but over a much longer period of time. During ice formation, layers build on top of each other. This exerts great pressure on the ice below. Eventually this pressure becomes so great, that the edges of the ice begin to shift. This movement is enhanced by gravity; glaciers on steep mountainsides experience greater movement than those on flatter land. The pressure also causes ice underneath the glacier to melt, which increases the movement.

▼ The Franz Josef glacier on New Zealand's South Island is around 7.5 miles (12 km) long. It flows from the Southern Alps into a temperate rain forest.

▲ This is the Half Dome in Yosemite National Park.

Material trapped in the ice, such as rock and gravel, rubs and erodes the surface over which the glacier travels. Some of the resulting scratches have been discovered and provide scientists with clues regarding glacier movement, including the direction of movement.

Glaciers also adhere to rock faces. As the glacier moves, it can tear away massive chunks of rock. For example, a glacier carried away much of the colossal Half Dome rock in Yosemite National Park.

Entire valleys are shaped by glaciers through abrasion and erosion. Even today, we see this at work. The Rhône Valley in Switzerland continues to be shaped by a slow-moving strip of ice.

DID YOU KNOW?

▶ Some glaciers in Greenland can travel several miles a year.
▶ Scientists believe that the most severe glaciation, or ice age, occurred between 580 million and 750 million years ago. Ice covered the entire planet, creating a "snowball earth." Even the oceans were completely frozen.

6

The driest places on the earth

Most deserts receive less than 10 inches (25 cm) of rainfall per year. The rain may fall all at once or sporadically. Some deserts go through years with no rain at all. Deserts cover about 30 percent of the earth's surface. The largest desert is the Sahara Desert in North Africa. It covers 3.5 million square miles (9,065,000 sq km), which is roughly the same size as the U.S.

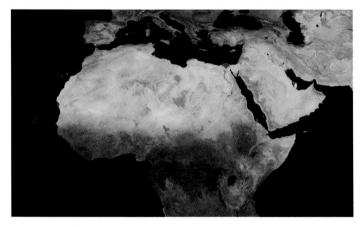

▲ The Sahara Desert can be seen from space.

TYPES OF DESERTS

Deserts are classified according to many factors, such as the number of days of rainfall, temperature, humidity, location, and wind. Some types of deserts are described here:

HOT AND DRY DESERTS

For most of the year, these deserts are warm during the day but sweltering in the summer months. There is little rainfall, and humidity is very low. At night, the lack of water vapor in the atmosphere allows heat to escape, and the temperature can plummet as low as 0°F (-18°C).

Rainfall in hot and dry deserts occurs in short bursts, between long periods of drought. Because the ground is so hot, evaporation occurs at a faster rate than the rain can fall. Some rain even evaporates before it hits the ground. An example of this type of desert is the Sahara Desert in North Africa, which receives only 0.6 inches (1.5 cm) of rain per year.

TRADE WIND DESERTS

The trade winds blow toward the equator from the northern and southern hemispheres. The winds are hot and dry, and they remove the cloud cover over latitudinal regions 30° north and south of the equator. This allows more of the sun's energy to heat the land. The Sahara Desert is formed by the trade winds.

▼ The trade winds blow toward the equator and create very dry regions.

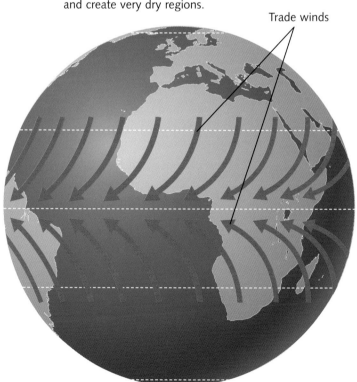

Trade winds

SEMIARID DESERTS

Semiarid deserts receive between 9.8 and 19.6 inches (25–50 cm) of rain each year and are found in North America, Europe, and northern Asia. The summers are long and dry, and the winters have very little rain. In fact, precipitation is mostly in the form of snow at high elevations. The temperature varies between 50°F and 80.6°F (10°C–27°C). Dew forms during the night, supplementing the rain.

COASTAL DESERTS

These deserts are located on the western edges of continents, such as Chile, western Australia, and southwestern Africa. Coastal deserts are not hot. They have cool winters, warm summers, and little rainfall. Their formation is caused by a complex interaction between oceanic, atmospheric, and terrestrial (land-related) systems.

RAIN-SHADOW DESERTS

These deserts form when tall mountains prevent moisture-rich clouds from reaching the far side of the mountains. As moist air rises over the mountains, the water vapor condenses into clouds. Eventually it falls on the tops of the mountains either as rain or snow, leaving the far side dry. The Himalayas play an important part in the formation of deserts in central Asia, such as the Taklimakan and Gobi deserts.

MONSOON DESERTS

If there is a large temperature difference between a continent and the surrounding ocean, a monsoon wind will result. Monsoon winds are strong. The monsoon patterns around India are responsible for pouring a deluge of rain on the land in short periods of time. As large amounts of rain fall in one place, another region often suffers from a lack of rain, which causes deserts to form. The Thar Desert in Pakistan and India is an example of a monsoon desert.

COLD DESERTS

These deserts have an annual rainfall between 6 and 10 inches (15–26 cm), and their summer temperature is rarely above 50°F (10°C). They have short summers followed by long, cold winters. Cold deserts, also called polar deserts, cover more than 2 million square miles (5 million sq km) of the earth. They are found in the Antarctic and the Arctic, which includes parts of the U.S., Canada, Russia, Norway, Sweden, Finland, and Iceland. They are either covered by ice and snow, or they are tundra—tundra landscapes are treeless plains that remain frozen for much of the year.

▼ This coastal tundra is on the island of Fugloya, about 500 miles (800 km) north of Norway.

HOW DO DESERTS FORM?

Desertification happens when fertile land becomes desert. Deserts expand and recede as a result of natural processes over thousands of years, but the actions of humans can accelerate desert formation:

(1) When land is overgrazed, or overused, plant life is lost.

(2) Plants hold soil together; once plants are gone, the land is more susceptible to erosion by wind and rain.

(3) Erosion removes the top layer of soil.

(4) There are few trees providing shade in areas undergoing desertification. This increases the evaporation rate of water, which draws salt from the earth to the surface soil.

(5) The salt prevents additional plant life from growing.

Desertification is particularly widespread in China. China's rural human and livestock populations have greatly increased over the last 60 years. The Gobi Desert is expanding at a rate of 950 square miles (2,460 sq km) per year, and massive dust storms are becoming more frequent. To counteract this desertification, the government plans to install a "Green Wall" of trees in northeastern China. The wall will be 3,542 miles (5,700 km) long, much longer than the famous Great Wall of China. Chinese officials say that by the year 2050, much of the arid land will be restored. But others are less hopeful. They say that reforestation will not work because many of the trees will die, and those that survive will absorb large amounts of water, which could increase desertification.

▼ Approximately 1.1 million tons (1 million t) of Gobi Desert sand blows into Beijing, China, each year.

DID YOU KNOW?

▶ China has both the highest and lowest deserts in the world. The Qaidam Basin is found at 8,530 feet (2,600 m) above sea level and the Turpan Basin is 492 feet (150 m) below sea level.

▶ The Atacama Desert in Chile is the driest place on the earth. It receives rain only once every 5 to 20 years.

TEST YOURSELF

How would you classify the following deserts? Use the clues to help you to decide.

▶ Death Valley. This desert is surrounded by the Black Mountains.
▶ Antarctica. Here, the temperature is very low all year.
▶ Deserts of Utah, Montana, and Nevada. Summers here are long, but winters can bring rain.

Death Valley National Park is a rain-shadow desert and receives less than 20 inches (50 cm) of rain per year. It is certainly the hottest, driest place in the U.S. The highest recorded temperature was a staggering 135.7°F (56.7°C) and the lowest recorded temperature was 15°F (–9.4°C).

FORMATION OF THE VALLEY

The oldest rock in Death Valley is 1.7 million years old and formed at a time when life on the earth was restricted to single-celled organisms, such as bacteria. Between 800 million and 1.2 billion years ago, marine deposition occurred. The western U.S. was a warm and tropical sea. When the clams, snails, and starfish that lived in the sea died, they fell to the sea floor and mixed with sand and silt. After 350 million years, 3.7 miles (6 km) of sediment had been deposited. Many of the exposed rocks in Death Valley were formed by these marine creatures, and it is not unusual to find fossils from this era.

VOLCANOES AND MOUNTAINS

The next stage in the formation of Death Valley was one of the most dramatic. Between 65 million and 250 million years ago, subduction occurred on the western side of the valley. High temperatures and immense pressures melted the rock. Some of the magma cooled beneath the surface and formed the intrusive igneous rock, granite. Some magma erupted through the earth's surface and formed lava flows that can still be seen today. The lava formed extrusive igneous rock that contained precious minerals, such as gold and silver.

▼ **Ancient lava flow in Death Valley.**

EROSION AND SPREADING

The volcanoes and mountains from this era were eroded over millions of years. Approximately 16 million years ago, the North American crust began to spread apart. Between two and three million years ago, the stretching reached the Death Valley area and formed the Death Valley basin. The basin filled with sediment—washed down from the surrounding mountains—and during the ice ages, it filled with water. Around 10,500 years ago, the valley was separated from the melted glacial waters in the Sierra Nevada mountains, and the desert formed.

DEATH VALLEY TODAY

At 282 feet (86 m) below sea level, the Badwater Basin in Death Valley is the lowest point in the western hemisphere. It contains minerals washed down from the surrounding mountains and salt from the evaporation of ancient lakes. The earth's crust in this area is still spreading, and no one knows for certain how this area will look thousands of years from now.

▼ **The salt-encrusted Death Valley basin.**

Glossary

CONDENSE – To change from a gas to a liquid.

CONSERVATIVE BOUNDARY – A boundary between plates where crust is neither formed nor destroyed.

CONSTRUCTIVE BOUNDARY – Boundary between plates where new crust material is formed.

CONTINENTAL DRIFT – Movement of oceanic or continental plates on the earth's surface.

CONTINENTAL PLATE – A plate that forms the earth's continents. One plate may be partly continental and partly oceanic.

CONVECTION CURRENT – Movement created by hot material rising, cooling, and then falling again.

DESTRUCTIVE BOUNDARY – Boundary between plates where crust material is destroyed.

EROSION – The wearing away of land through natural processes, such as water, wind, ice, or gravity.

GEOLOGIST – A person who studies the science of the earth.

GREENHOUSE EFFECT – The warming of a planet caused by greenhouse gases that prevent heat from escaping into space.

IGNEOUS ROCK – Rock formed from cooling molten magma.

KELVIN – A unit of temperature. Zero Kelvin is called absolute zero and is equal to -459.67°F (-273.15°C).

LAVA – Molten magma that is expelled from a volcano.

MAGMA – Molten rock beneath the earth's surface.

METAMORPHIC ROCK – Rock formed under intense heat and pressure.

NUCLEAR FUSION – Joining of nuclei.

OCEANIC PLATE – A plate that forms the earth's surface under the oceans.

OSMOSIS – Movement of a solvent, through a semipermeable membrane, from an area where there is a lot of it to an area where there is little.

ANSWERS

Page 9: Test yourself
Layers of sediment are formed in three ways.
1. When the weathered remains of other rocks are deposited.

2. When the remains of plants and animals. are deposited.

3. When the liquid part of a solution, such as seawater, evaporates to leave behind a layer of sediment.

The layers build on top of one another and become compressed to form sedimentary rock. Sedimentary rocks include coal (a biogenic sedimentary rock), halite (a precipitate sedimentary rock), and sandstone (neither biogenic nor precipitate).

Page 13: Test yourself
Igneous rocks form when magma (molten rock) from beneath the earth's surface cools and solidifies. The rock can cool underground or above the ground.

When rock cools underground it is called intrusive igneous rock. It cools because it moves toward the cooler surface of the earth, but does not break through the surface.

When rock cools above the ground it is called extrusive igneous rock. It cools because it has been expelled from under the ground, often through a volcano, where it meets cooler air or water.

Page 19: Investigate
Porous rock contains tiny holes, or pores. Nonporous rock does not have pores. Nonporous rock is better for building because it is less susceptible to erosion by wind, rain, and chemicals.

Page 21: Test yourself
Red layers can clearly be seen in the photograph. These sections contain a lot of iron that has leached from surrounding rocks.

White layers can also be observed. These are rich in limestone (calcium carbonate) formed from dead sea animals.

PHOTOSYNTHESIS – The process during which green plants use sunlight to convert carbon dioxide and water into energy and oxygen.

PLASMA – An extremely hot gas that is composed of atomic nuclei without electrons and free electrons.

PLATE BOUNDARY – Where two tectonic plates meet.

PLATE TECTONICS – The theory that the earth's crust is made of plates that float on the earth's molten interior.

RECRYSTALLIZATION – When atoms or molecules of a rock or mineral are packed close together to create a new crystal structure. This usually occurs under conditions of intense temperature and pressure.

RICHTER SCALE – A measure of earthquake strength on a scale from 0 to 10. This is a logarithmic scale. This means that a magnitude 7 earthquake is ten times more powerful than a magnitude 6 earthquake.

SALINITY – A measure of the amount of salt dissolved in water.

SEDIMENTARY ROCK – Rock made from millions of tiny sediments.

SEMIPERMEABLE MEMBRANE – A membrane that allows only certain substances to pass through it.

SUBDUCTION – When one tectonic plate passes under another tectonic plate.

SUBLIME – To turn directly from a solid into a gas, or vice versa.

SUPERNOVA – The explosion of a massive star at the end of its life.

TRANSPORTATION – The movement of small sediment material to alternative locations through natural processes.

WEATHERING – The breakdown of rock through physical, chemical, or biological processes.

Useful Web sites:
http://www.chem4kids.com
http://www.howstuffworks.com
http://www.dustbunny.com/afk/index.html
http://education.usgs.gov/common/secondary.html
http://www.newscientist.com

Page 31: Investigate
The water on the plate should not taste salty.

The salty water has boiled and steam has formed. Steam is the evaporation product of the salt water. Steam contains only water molecules and no salt molecules. The salt remains in the pan.

If the pan is left in a warm place, eventually all of the water will evaporate and only salt crystals will remain.

Page 33: Investigate
Example answers:
Constructive boundary—The Great Rift Valley has formed as a result of the separation of the African and Arabian tectonic plates. It is 3,107 miles (5,000 km) long and runs from northern Syria in southwest Asia to central Mozambique in east Africa. The Arabian plate and two parts of the African plate—the Nubian and the Somalian—are moving away from each other.

Destructive boundary—The Andes Mountains have formed as a result of the collision between the Nazca Plate and the South American Plate.

Conservative boundary—The boundary between the Pacific Plate and the North American Plate is conservative. The Pacific Plate is pushing north and the North American Plate is pushing south. It has created the San Andreas Fault, which runs 800 miles (1,287 km) through western and southern California in the U.S.

Page 44: Test yourself
Death Valley is a rain-shadow desert because it is surrounded by the Black Mountains.

Antarctica is a cold, or polar, desert because the temperatures are very low.

The deserts of Utah, Montana, and Nevada are semiarid because the summers are long and hot, but winters bring rain. They receive slightly more rain than hot deserts.

Index

Photo Credits – (abbv: r, right, l, left, t, top, m, middle, b, bottom, c, center) **Cover background image** www.istockphoto.com/Ryan Johnson **Front cover images** (bl) www.istockphoto.com/Mike Morley (br) www.istockphoto.com/Zoe Funnell **Back cover image** www.istockphoto.com/Mike Morley **p.1** (bl) www.istockphoto.com/Kent Steffens (br) www.istockphoto.com/Ryan Johnson (tr) www.istockphoto.com/Will Louie **p.2** Jean-Pierre Lescourret/Corbis **p.3** (t) www.istockphoto.com/Pam Jeffries (b) www.istockphoto.com/Ron Sumners **p.4** (lc) www.istockphoto.com/Zoe Funnell (tr) www.istockphoto.com/Norbert Rohr (br) B. Murton/ Southampton Oceanography Centre/Science Photo Library **p.5** Jeremy Walker/Science Photo Library **p.7** (b) NASA, Andrew Fruchter and the ERO Team [Sylvia Baggett (STScI), Richard Hook (ST-ECF), Zoltan Levay (STScI)] **p.8** www.istockphoto.com/Vera Bogaerts **p.9** www.istockphoto.com/Pam Jeffries **p.10** www.istockphoto.com/Nicolas Metivier **p.11** (tr) Russ Munn/Agstocksua/Science Photo Library (tm) Andrew Lambert Photography/Science Photo Library (tl) Andrew Lambert Photography/Science Photo Library (mc) www.istockphoto.com/Marek Slusarczyk (b) www.istockphoto.com/Steve Geer **p.13** (t) www.istockphoto.com/Dave Jilek, (b) www.istockphoto.com/Allan Brown **p.14** (l) www.istockphoto.com/Andrew Green (r) www.istockphoto.com/Kelly Borsheim **p.15** (tl) www.istockphoto.com/Will Louie (br) www.istockphoto.com/Vera Bogaerts **p.16** (t) Duncan Shaw/Science Photo Library (b) Sinclair Stammers/Science Photo Library **p.17** www.istockphoto.com/Zoe Funnell **p.18** Bernhard Edmaier/SCIENCE PHOTO LIBRARY **p.20** Jean-Pierre Lescourret/Corbis **p.20** www.istockphoto.com/Jason Cheever **p.22** Charles D. Winters/Science Photo Library **p.23** P.G. Adam, Publiphoto Diffusion/Science Photo Library **p.25** Bildagentur-Online/TH_Foto/Science Photo Library **p.26** NASA Marshall Space Flight Center (NASA-MSFC) **p.27** (t) B. Murton/ Southampton Oceanography Centre/Science Photo Library (b) Courtesy NASA/JPL-Caltech **p.28** (bl) Crown Copyright/Health & Safety Laboratory/Science Photo Library (tr) Richard Folwell/Science Photo Library **p.29** Alison Wright/CORBIS **p.30** www.istockphoto.com/Norbert Rohr **p.31** (t) www.istockphoto.com/Ulrike Hammerich (br) Ria Novosti/Science Photo Library **p.37** Evan Schneider/epa/Corbis **p.39** Evan Schneider/epa/Corbis **p.39** www.istockphoto.com/Bogdan Lazar (b) Alberto Garcia/Corbis **p.40** Jeremy Walker/Science Photo Library **p.41** www.istockphoto.com/Trevor Buttery **p.42** (t) NASA Earth Observatory **p.43** Simon Fraser/Science Photo Library **p.44** Reuters/CORBIS **p.45** (l) www.istockphoto.com/Ryan Johnson (r) www.istockphoto.com/Steve Geer